SPRING MEDITATION

SPRING MEDITATION

KEVIN MILLER

MoonPath Press

Copyright © 2022 Kevin Miller
All rights reserved.

No part of this publication may be reproduced, distributed, or transmitted in any form or by any means whatsoever without written permission from the publisher, except in the case of brief excerpts for critical reviews and articles. All inquiries should be addressed to MoonPath Press.

Poetry
ISBN 978-1-936657-66-7

Cover art by Kelda Martensen
Cover art inset photo: 1928, Jack Miller,
Nob Hill Ave N, Seattle. WA

Author photo by Cameon Miller

Book design by Tonya Namura, using Garamond Premier Pro

MoonPath Press, an imprint of Concrete Wolf Poetry Series,
is dedicated to publishing the finest poets
living in the U.S. Pacific Northwest.

MoonPath Press
PO Box 445
Tillamook, OR 97141

MoonPathPress@gmail.com

http://MoonPathPress.com

For Mike Shannon, Editor
*Spitball: The Literary
Baseball Magazine*

Baseball is like church.
Many attend, few understand.

—Leo Durocher

Contents

Hike with My Father in Mind	3
The Minors	4
Curve Ball	5
The Heart for Hang Time	6
At the Ball Field Across From the Arletta Store	7
Baseball Weather	8
I See You and the Short Porch	9
Intentional Pass	10
A Picture of Eudora Welty	12
This One Time	13
The Battery in October	14
Eighth Grade Spring	15
Non-League Play	16
McNeil Island Penitentiary Closes	18
Spring Meditation	19
After the Ball Is Over	20
Hoist with Our Own Bédard	21
Away	22
No Pilgrim, No Pilgrimage	24
Head Games	25
The Man With No Church	26
From This Angle	28
Wins and Losses	29
Sea Level	30
The Marquee at the Blue Mouse	31

You Can't Argue Balls and Strikes	32
Poem for Edwin on the DL	34
The National Pastime	35
Note to Edwin after Cancellation of the 2020 Minor League Season	37
Ravens, Fathers & Sons	38
What Stopped You for Years	39
No Substitute for Winter	40
Another at Bat	41
Cabin Visitation, Flagermus	42
Looking Out this Window Thinking of Ernie Banks and William Carlos Williams	43
Acknowledgements	45
Gratitude	47
About the Author	49

SPRING MEDITATION

Hike with My Father in Mind

Mt. Rainier, Washington

My father hated the Boy Scouts,
something to do with men and
boys in the same tent, distrust
of anyone who refused sports.
I learned to block the curve ball
in the dirt, take it off my chest
and keep it ready to play.
Building a fire in any weather
was beyond my practice.
No man in the woods is saved
by his ability to handle the short
hop, framing a pitch does little
for a one's sense of direction.
My experience with bears was
the Yakima Bears, the only stars
I can name are the Mick, Roger,
and Yogi. I was taught to revere
constellations like Satchel and Jackie.
No hiker ever found his way to safety
following Van Lingle Mungo
in the night sky. Still, I persist
on the trail to Spray Park, the bugs
and dust nothing when you know
how to take one for the team.

The Minors

Those birds were not enough
to save me, the darting blips
out the corner of the eye failed
to help me pick up the seams.

I walked home from practice
eating dime-bag Fritos, counting
nests hidden in the cemetery hedge,
my stories all laurel and robins

carried to the dinner table, late
again. *Feather merchant*, Dad
said, every player at table fixed
with a moniker fit for a dugout.

Our chore instructions echoed
a play by play the field marshal
chipped, *Eye on the ball, Choke up,
Step to the pitch,* a manager's call.

This edge should be like *a frozen
rope, cut two and turn to right,*
slight variations to fit the duties
of the yard— while he mowed

shirtless in shorts. He always said,
*If you don't make it between
the lines, you can have a career
working with the grounds crew.*

Curve Ball

On McCarver, the manhole cover
even with the front window lines
up perfectly with each passing car
and when they wed, the rubber
and steal shudder a solid clank,
and if you notice it once,
you own it over and over,
five seconds from the stop sign
so you are ready and waiting
and if it fails to go off,
you wonder if they are drunk
or stopping by for a visit
before they head north
toward Vashon, a step-stone
to Seattle where your dogs are buried,
where an uncle walked home
from the downtown library every day,
where Jim Mjelde, a one-armed kid
pitched in little league and your father
went to battle with coaches
who cut him from the all-star team
because Jim broke too many bats.
Those bastards are long dead,
and when the next car bah-thumps,
you are eleven, Jim's on the mound,
his mitt stuck under the stub.
He releases a 12-6 curve bound to settle
into your glove like rubber to metal.

The Heart for Hang Time

for B.C.M.

On the side yard, catch
eased to flies and grounders.
Grounders on grass so torn
meant unpredictable hops,
turns in direction no father
controlled. At home,
before fungoes and warning
tracks, you begged higher,
higher, and I dipped what was left
of an already tired arm to find
an angle to challenge you.
It was always that hang time
I could not handle, those moments
not knowing whether what I set
in motion was blessing or curse.
I favor catchers over pitchers,
prefer soft hands to muscle.
I find comfort in knowing
you have the good first step,
you are all grace in the sun field.

At the Ball Field Across From the Arletta Store

When the light is right
the time when day feels
tired but not asleep,
when no one is hurried
save the bats, the lines
and shapes of one day
drift slowly into the blank
of tomorrow. Today
someone left a white chair
along the first baseline.
The store is closed, the Arletta
Yankees have been driven home.
They dream. No one sits
and watches the empty field.

Baseball Weather

I read over and over things not written
in the letter. He writes, *Watch the Yankees.*
I look for his wife's name, try to read his life at home.
No words place her in a room, I find no place
for her to walk up a step, no coat on a banister,
no faces stay in the house I make for him, nothing
in the house that he does not mention in his last letter.
When he writes, it could be weather,
this baseball, and books. No blood in the scores.
A year ago he wrote people who died.
He never mentioned names, I imagined them, short
one syllable given names, three syllable surnames,
faces with tired eyes, families in wooden pews.
People like the people I brush against every day.
Here, we hold the space he leaves in the letter
over a candle in the kitchen, our power gone
to a storm three thousand miles west of his storm.
What cellar protects us from what he fails to write,
what distance twists her out of the language?
One morning I see her pour milk over cereal,
another he stacks books under an arm, turns
up his collar, leaves an empty house for a classroom
full of the lives he uses to hold the love left.

I See You and the Short Porch

at Howe Field with the Lynx
and days when a good stretch
meant a splits-defining reach
to save a one-hop fade halfway
to out, or worse a throw that falls
short and comes up cuffs on the rise
as if the elevator on this stretch
went both ways, days when scoop
had nothing to do with ice cream
or journalism or Everett's Senator.
From today on, it's the soft hands
cupping the mail, the new strength
in steps back along the river, an ease
as smooth as the new Cadillac strut.

Intentional Pass

Early in his career, sliding late,
my father broke his leg
and was forced to take
practice swings with a clarinet.

He did steal, struck hot pies
cooling safe on a sill.
Like hanging curves, they enticed
a double play, Don Mason to Dad,
Tinker to Evers, but
chance would have it, they erred,
caught behind cabin four
and released from summer camp.

In thirty-four, at sixteen
on the road with the Yakima Legion,
Johnny Miller swung late,
lined an outside fastball,
a rope to right. Legend has it
rolling past the right fielder
over the bank.
Damn thing rolled all the way
to downtown Naches.
I mean it.
He meant it.

This summer at five a.m.
I drive through Yakima.
My family sleeps as first light
shows *Naches 1 Mile*.
Should I check the pitch
of that right field bank,
pace the distance downtown?

I play the percentages,
give Naches an intentional pass,
and over breakfast tell my son
and daughter of their grandfather's
habit to take it to right.

A Picture of Eudora Welty

This is the March that follows no winter.
Already mosquitoes own left field.
A new kid wants to pitch but not attend class.
A legend from Spokane signs for thirty-one million.
Welty knows about cheap seats;
she knows a story will save our lives.
Stories keep us young.
Give me the right woman in a porch rocker
over any experienced bull pen.

This One Time

As boys we had team cards.
Men stood in pinstriped tiers.
They held our places as we smacked the ball
against the side of the garage and turned
deep to the hole, all the hops true, every throw
beats the runner by a step. I see you, right-handed
this one time, playing short, watching Norm Cash
stretch to pull it in. Freehan's the first to the dugout,
shouts, *Nice throw*, and Kaline gives you a pat
on the back that says everything left unsaid
in your ongoing play by play.
You make a new toss. It's already the next inning.

The Battery in October

When we conference on the mound,
this left-hander tells me Jane Gallagher
grew up and became Nancy Griffith.
I'm here to talk placement, thinking fastballs
out of the strike zone and off-speed
stuff, starting out and staying out.
We are too old for heat, too tired
for power after power.
Our game knows no lucky strikes.
The speeds we change may be misnamed.
Nothing means as much as finding Jane.

Each year the season runs closer to winter.
Strong hitters look nothing like Killebrew.
The heart of the order is so young. We still
push it in close to set up away, and we
know all the weaknesses worth knowing.
Before I return behind the plate, I mention
the woman who translates Fujii Yoshiyasu.
Lefty recites:
> *When the gate of my house is open,*
> *you can see a green mountain.*
> *If you don't mind being lonely,*
> *you are welcome anytime.*

No one hurries us.
Jane's in Austin.
We've got two outs,
the wind's blowing in from right.

Eighth Grade Spring

One son falling is no end,
salvation swings both ways.
The crucifix crosses
nuns in motion.
Sister heads west,
and Jesus, like clockwork,
heads east, his tiny chrome feet
soldered one over the other.
His hands point to sky and earth
ready to cartwheel for us all,
his station airy in its tumbling
before black habit crossing,
playground, or classroom.
Sister O's swinging for fences,
snapping rulers, correcting tenses.
No mistake's mortal
until spring sun pushes freckles
across the low throat of one girl.
Pray for skin's perfect patterned falling.
Give forgiveness a place to stay.

Non-League Play

for Seamus, Liam, Finnian, Maeve, Colm, and Sullivan

The skaters at Garfield Park favor
the bench near the cannon.
They are shooting stars grinding
chrome tails across the green metal seat.
Boys with no taste for Little League
or soccer play follow the leader
on the Wright Academy tennis courts.
They hang the helmets mothers demand
on net standards as they pump and glide,
segments of a stretching snake
winding in and out of bounds.
No one calls anyone about playing time.

On the infield, three girls work a golden
retriever in an equilateral romp for a Frisbee.
He wears a scarf bib and tosses
his head on the way to return the disk.
The girl near second and heading to right
makes an over the shoulder grab,
her grace a silent Say-Hey ballet.

Hacky sackers slacking in cottonwood shade
mime bicycle riding in quick kicking spurts
as they keep what is soft aloft. A new kid arrives,
the circle widens. No timeouts, no coaches
to make ceremony or ritual of substitutions.
Everybody plays as long as he likes.

The grandfather near the slides
watches his grandson run away
from the play toys, heading for the dog.
Midway, the boy stomps white clover.
He changes direction, chases bees, on his way-
ward path through these minor leagues.

McNeil Island Penitentiary Closes

The island boat sails
empty one way. For
years I told the kids
of our away games
against fed inmates,
the Native pitcher
with hand-carved knives
tattooed underside
his forearms, his stare
walleyed as searchlights
when a kid sixteen
brushed him back. He eyed
me with unwieldy
daggers, safe behind
horizontal bars,
I squatted, signaled
for a curve. Bleacher
bums hooted, howled,
and bet cigarettes
on each pitch. One guy
yelled, *He killed seven
guys, watch your back
at the plate.* Hitters
joked about playing
the next game at our place.
We split the double-
header and ate lunch
at the big house.

Spring Meditation

short toss with Wiffle balls—
the elder brother shags,
the younger swings
the bulbous blue bat,
spins half circle
and falls on wet grass.
The grandfather on one knee
recalls his start, all three
hit southpaw, the turn
to short toss is method,
a step back for contact,
head-hands-eyes
as simple as breath,
and he recalls Gary Schwab
placing a bat behind his foot
to force his step to the pitch,
forget Gordy Coleman,
he holds the ball still,
has the boy swing
to the point of impact,
stop, feel the extension,
extend—*it means
your arms look like this V,*
he rises, holds the boy's hips
to show open, belly button
to the pitcher, he remembers
Connie Hamilton telling
a kid *Squeeze your cheeks,
imagine holding a fiver,*
first soft toss a line shot
sticks a blue moon
in the laurel hedge.

After the Ball Is Over

In the North End I pass the lefty
who threw crossfire fastballs
for the Cougars on the Palouse
thirty-five years ago.
While he combs the yard for twigs
and leaves, his edger and mower
sport tags from the shop,
ready for the season opener.
He's kept a sure step and balance,
though he looks slow to his left,
he'll need the back hand
to stop the leaf near the curb.

He wears the V-neck slicker of a pitcher
about to hit fungoes, his gray sweats
could be flannels, he shows some sock.
The drag bunt up the line is the best shot
to pass before he makes his cut.
His mowing pattern is a straight-line grid,
parking strip lines east-west, no fancy
infield cross, though he crosses the line
to keep his edge, this green goes deep,
shows signs of foreign substances.

Hoist with Our Own Bédard

Tillman kills us again,
keeps his perfect record,
the agony of all things
Bédard lingers and fills
a room the way a fresh
blast of analgesic balm
restores fire to the agony
of the lefty who refused
to ruffle his shirt or risk
breaking a sweat, whose
time on the disabled list
accrued in dog years.
Still after Tillman peppers
the wound with salt, one
Adam Jones shows his class
as a force at the plate,
the leader of outfield and
clubhouse, while Seattle
fans are left knowing each
wasted buck is a buck
forty in Canada.

Away

for Clark Babbitt and Connie Hamilton, r.i.p.

Road trip— the college station wagons
cross the mountains and head
to the dry side of the state.
No one's fool enough to mistake
this for the big time, we are away
from the endless rain and wood
hovels where most of us live.
The eight dollars meal money
turns us into scholarship athletes.
First afternoon is an apple valley,
sun, heat, and the first infield outside
after weeks of fungoes on the gym floor.
We drop the nine-inning opener
to the community college boys
and pile into the white wagons
mouthing excuses, the unearned rest.
By evening we cross into Idaho.
The hotel is crime fiction,
hammering on exposed pipes is real,
hot water imagined. Upper classmen
secret us across state lines to Washington
for beers while the coaches aim for the heart
of downtown for pizza and drink.
Two pitchers unable to find a corner
or common sense have already settled
in the heart of the heart with cigarettes and beers.
0 and 1, they fail the discretion test.
They start next day's double-header running
foul lines outside the windscreen fence.
By the middle of the fifth, we take bets
as Torres stumbles and slumps.
He's laps behind Babbitt who continues

to make a movement resembling a jog.
The road trip slamming continues—
home-half innings take forever.
The bench boys of this losing team hide
snickers behind gloves and unused helmets.
It's eighty and so muggy the air is butter.
Bets errantly favor mercy in game two.
Our assistant coach delivers water, the banished
continue left   center   right   and back.
The season is young, we are 0 and 2.
Fifth inning of game three, we're up four.
Coach sends the backup catcher for the boys.
Bottom of the seventh, two on, up one, one out.
Coach Hamilton calls time, walks out to stall.
Babbitt's down the first baseline throwing.
Hamilton waves him to the mound,
Babbitt retires two, we are 1 and 2.
Back on the road, it's all uphill,
the Lewiston Grade heading to Pullman
and the too short lives each had left.

No Pilgrim, No Pilgrimage

for C.F.

You have a mind of winter
finding your way from this coast
to Connecticut walking knee deep
in the flawed master's snow.
My brother, now a man, sports
his JP Patches tee shirt—
the face of the TV clown worn
like a scapular in short, Seattle days.
The custodian who claims to hate kids
does a great Bart when he says, *Cool*.
Winter light keeps falling from the sky,
Otis Redding fifty-four Decembers gone.
To understand is to mark their steps
for others, like two boys from Hibbing,
Zimmerman and Maris with hit records
and record hits— sung and unsung.

Head Games

Hours throwing a tennis ball
against our garage door,
good and bad hops spray
the driveway, Leo Lassen's
play by play and my color
splice generations of players,
say Jimmy Foxx, the Mick,
Gordy Coleman, Jungle Jim
Rivera, Richard Mark, assorted
icons, lesser and un-knowns team
for a 9th Avenue double-header.
The left field line is a driveway wall
eight feet from right's concrete
other—good hands surpass range.
Velocity and carom keep me honest.
The next pitch might strike the trip
at the garage door's center, render
a weak pop fly past the oil fill-pipe.
This stays—I refuse to cheat.
When I kick a backhand grab,
or a bobble takes an extra second
from pocket to throw, the boot
runs the game into extra innings.
No games are called for rain,
some extend in streetlights' haze,
others end suddenly after Mom's
third call out the front door grate.

The Man With No Church

has friends who pick stones
from three rivers,
devotion & discovery
finds the assorted spread
around their driveway—
will man bring home bees
to keep honey close?
The gods contradict,
I don't have the stones
to say let sleeping rocks lie.

The radios says
Mercer Island people
must boil their water,
employment will rise,
some may find a stove
in a kitchen where water
and fire come together
for the first time.

This morning the alley
is filled with apples,
I think Henry-up-the-way
continues to train for his
future in white crime,
stick-fights the ceremony
his little league plays.

Four a.m. coffee, *her* cup,
as if what cup matters,
fog, yesterday's accusations
no better than blame,
my neighbor a few years

beyond his pitch count
finds neither strike zone
nor fat raccoons feasting
in his grape arbor, how
do I like them apples.

From This Angle

I say Sonny Liston, she hears sunny disposition.
She lives in night. I walk the dark of morning.
Our silences bump into each other.

One cloud through another is mist.
Her Mozart lingers beneath Coltrane.
She tells me of Teresa of Ávila, her heart in glass.

At my desk, Roberto Clemente wears Pirate black.
He stays in the air, his plane forever ascending.
Our icons are sovereign flags.

We fall to each other in isosceles dependence,
our baseline weighted with accidents and opposites,
saints and complaints. She hates crowd noise on TV.

I think the way in is the suicide squeeze, the way out
a fast ball behind the head. No instinct tells us lean in.
The finger meant to type *trace* makes *grace*.

Crows' racket calls the eye, these black dots
an ellipsis to the red tail atop the neighbor's pine.
Some wrong numbers last a lifetime.

The photo I think is my daughter turns
into her mother fourteen years before the knock
at my door. Sneakers in the dryer are kettle drums,

and Allie is every lost love whose allegiance
we long to keep. What could be better, this game
and all our favorite lines on the inside of our mitts.

Wins and Losses

How long between breaths,
anger takes you by the throat,
logic and clarity are color,
to keep breathing, a victory,
seeing red is the day's backdrop,
a friend's bloody hell says it,
chest thumping boiled blood,
simply pudding, you seek
the seam to slip from yourself,
the forgiveness of sins you
once repeated, and if no sins
exist, seething appears, reminds
you they have made names
for these actions like mad
before dog, heart-snarl flecks
of saliva, hunchback crooked
walk, if this is not sin then surely
a switch across your snout, a prod
wired with a truth forgotten,
you once favored a child counting
robins' nests in laurel hedges
around the cemetery where your
parents are buried, the way to see
through, to follow a song, when
fear meant an occasional hawk
and trouble home late for supper
because of birds after baseball.

Sea Level

The lake stories involved alligators
rising from sewers or worse, tales
of swimming in a puree of city bilge
our father promised us whenever
we whined about the temperature
of the Sound, its jellyfish and barnacles.
Seaweed rafts settled like blanket
satin at the shore, required the family's
traditional running leap and dive.
We took it for gospel, considered
three strokes swimming, relished
low tide and the bliss as in-tide washed
over heated sand. We lived our lives
in the shadow of a majestic mountain
and knew it no closer than the beer can.
The family Kool-Aid favored baseball
over boy scouts, hockey to skiing.
We supported the underdog, honored
picket lines, drove Chevs never Fords.
We used the public library and never
wore our religion on our sleeves.

The Marquee at the Blue Mouse

announces *42*, and my grandson says
he wants to see Babe Ruth, quicker
than I can say Jack Robinson, I am
fourteen playing Babe Ruth League
holding the thick handled Hillerich
& Bradsby / Jackie Robinson 34,
and it's too much to explain, I slip
to others, Smokey, Swiss Family,
and Tom who faced Robert E. Ewell,
I pivot to Cano and Jeffers, I end
trying to tell Liam about my goldfish
Pee Wee Reese and Jackie who broke
the surface, left life in a fishbowl.

You Can't Argue Balls and Strikes

written during reigns of Benedict VI & Anton Scalia

it's like Scalia is behind the plate
and Thomas at first, sure as shit
the Pope and Seattle's Archbishop
are manning the other bases, done
deal, you wanna play? whattaya
lookin' at? in the land of the free,
there's no arguing, chump, don't
look sideways, there's no talking
to the man, the bully down the block
has your arms pinned, and he drops
orange-soda spit till it nearly touches
your face, then he sucks it back up,
laughs before he starts to pound
his knuckles into your chest,
the whole time your mind plays
reruns of war movies, you love
the French resistance, especially
bereted ones who don't get topped,
you see them at night, the ones
with the stars are what stars should be—
shooting, you savor each little victory
and you remember Half-Share,
a guy you caught in college, he's pissed
at the ump for squeezing him on the corners,
he calls you to the mound, says,
Signal curve, expect curve, stay down,
and you do just as he says, and he coils,
serves his best stuff, a lively heater
pops the sonofabitch right in the bars—
that'll wake 'em up, and now I am thinking
of a fastball for Scalia, an errant pick-off
play at first to deck Thomas

who's asking no questions
and still making bad calls,
a misguided double play connection
might jar the fecking Archbishop, still,
it will take an act of god to topple the Pope—
a line foul down third, remember Lasorda,
you can see those little red shoes flying
like scattered cardinals, around here
no one's packing the bats early.

Poem for Edwin on the DL

Riding the pines in September
takes patience, time is more
than first to third, or a heater's
clocking ninety-five plus.
Nothing subtle about late innings,
buddy, we are held together
with bailing wire and duct tape.
Analgesic balm is false hope
before it turns cold on the skin.
Yours is no Wally Pipp story,
we commit to hold your spot.
This game is pure beyond time,
it's Piersall, Gehrig, and Ernie's
Let's play two. Every day now
is extra innings, home and away.

The National Pastime

Once we were boys in love
with baseball, Ernie's *Let's play two*,

naïve save the story my father
shared about Jackie Robinson,

the day Kentucky's Pee Wee Reese
shows courage in Cincinnati.

We lived in a city of blue laws
and redlining, neighborhoods

kept separate like home and
away unis, whites always home.

The inside fastball was a great teacher.
Choking up meant Nellie Fox,

decades later it refers to this bile.
I am too old for ball, too late

for naiveté, this chilling echo—
the bully in chief returns to manage

our country, all fabrication
and faux gold, a mirror image

of Ben Chapman spewing epithets
I was dumb enough to think disappeared.

Chin music plays best with players,
cowards chip and hide in the dugout

emboldened by the dog's tight chain.
These red meat days, no one steals

this base with truth or rational thought.
I long for a bench-clearing brawl

to isolate the new Chapman cowering
in plain sight, that orange at the end

of the bench is not Gatorade.
I tell my grandsons how Lou Piniella

and his bat dealt with barrel-like-
orange-plastic things in a dugout.

Note to Edwin after Cancellation of the 2020 Minor League Season

Now that spitting is outlawed,
can scratching and cup lifting
moves be far behind? Who's
to say what new series of tics
will find the national pastime?
We only just decided Houston
had a problem, the hawk-eyed
thief always proved an asset.
And who'd bet against Pete's
ever persistent headfirst leap
toward the hall? Time wears us
down. When we battled over
masks, it was trying to get blue
to look between the bars,
now we can't keep the kids
out of them. For the Ms,
a shortened season is a plenary
indulgence, it abolishes purgatory
and sends us back to the beach.
Rainier tall cans vaccinate us
against the eternal failing rebuild.
We salute this version of a rainout,
savor the thought of Edgar safely
enshrined, and turn this L into a W.

Ravens, Fathers & Sons

My son and I talk raven visitations,
their daunting reach, their nods
at dusk, their *toks*, the anthracite beaks
worrying skylights like whetstones—

our shared reverence a verbal game
of catch for an old man and his middle-
aged son. We toss stories as we watch
the mystifying spectacle of lacrosse—

his fourth grader in hand-me-down
green gloves a young Hulk, his stick,
helmet and cage foreign to a man raised
on baseball, his son on soccer. We witness

the audible chop, the stick-to-stick clack.
My son asks his youngest the penalty
for slashing. *A minute.* My son responds,
How long could a minute be?

What Stopped You for Years

Nor is one silence equal to another
  —Donald Justice

What kept you from talking to the woman
at the market is a fence down. You wake
and high grass covers post holes,
tree lines fail to mark where things stop and start.
Kelly serves your coffee. You address her this once
by name. Even *Good Morning* wants a story.
You tell her the title of a book you wish you had read
at twenty-three. The man in the tweed cap
and windbreaker sits across from you for three years.
Every morning the two of you keep within your news.
Today, he speaks, something about Boston's late run,
and you mention Carlton Fisk. He turns half around
at this and says, *Buckner deserved so much better.*
He reminds you of Justice with those big glasses,
and you walk into your day recalling another man's
work and worth. You drive toward Ahtanum Ridge.
Three songs on the radio and you know someone
chooses their order—it's like listening to a line drawing,
the pen never lifts until black makes sense of white.
This morning has nothing to do with things given up.
You know five songs that could be next.

No Substitute for Winter

The thrush feasts on the half apple,
she's varied in the way the snowstorm

reveals secrets, wrapped the year
in rain gear. Wood-smoke rises

a line to a god, fog horns repeat
from bay waters south of Vashon.

The thrush's sable necklace reminds
us of things close, the way Brooks

Robinson calls to mind Gehrig,
Gehrig conjures Wally Pipp, and

while no substitute for an oriole,
in rain country we settle for close.

Fear of replacement haunts
like facing your doppelganger.

Song sparrows return after a day
of fox sparrows, as if the thaw

brings a thin wind. The woman
in snow pants will appear skinny-

jeaned and prancing. This Chinook
ushers the return of sneakers

and tee shirts. Three days pass
for winter, make way for robins.

Another at Bat

for Barry Grimes

The belfry's just another time at the plate,
no one keeps track of the misses, the swings

are as clean as we imagined, from the handle,
choked, or even the Jackie Robinson thick-

handled broom. We appreciate a good curve
where the bottom drops out, or the slider

given the demands of protected species.
We count our days knowing the good work

of others, knowing the river's the place a recent
hatch draws the maw from over and under.

What darts as dark appears, reminds us speed
without control is power, with luck we duck

the high hard one, we anticipate the change.

Cabin Visitation, Flagermus

in memory of John Julius Varga

The bats and broom stance
brings it back, the one crack
you have at it, make the most
of each swing, nothing casual
like take two and go to right,
this is an official at bat, it zags
at the open door, before what
may be your last chance this night
as light lives inside and not out,
your best John Varga inside-out
swing comes to mind, another thing
you never mastered as a player,
one you most appreciated while
catching as you called slider away,
John showed his off-field power
in silk degrees, he was the Boz,
his jazzy way with power, humble,
calm, while the septuagenarian puts
up another K, your QA Little League
days sixty years gone unlike the bat.

Looking Out this Window Thinking
of Ernie Banks and William Carlos Williams

The broken handled wheelbarrow leans
into its third spring, propped like
a knothole kid against the side fence.

The games go on, those of us benched
because of age understand quiet is
like a rainout, we pause to rebuild tired

arms, recover from losses, slumps, errors.
We have time to turn this thing around, rally.
The rookies are immortal, they laugh

and tip their caps from the end of the bench,
understanding part ritual and superstition.
We never pack the bats till the last out.

Acknowledgements

The author sincerely thanks the following publications where some of the poems in this collection previously appeared, sometimes in earlier versions:

Alkali Flats: "Baseball Weather"

Beyond Parallax: "At the Ballfield Across from the Arletta Store"

Fan: "The Heart for Hang Time"

Heart of the Order: Persea's Baseball Anthology: "McNeil Island Penitentiary Closes"

Spitball: "Cabin Visitation," "Away," "Spring Meditation," "Curve Ball," "McNeil Island Penitentiary Closes," "Hoist with Our Own Bédard," "Hike with My Father in Mind"

Spitball Poem of the Month: "Spring Meditation"

Several of the poems in this collection also appear in the author's other publications:

Light That Whispers Morning, Blue Begonia Press, 1994

Everywhere Was Far, Blue Begonia Press, 1998

Home & Away: The Old Town Poems, Pleasure Boat Studio, 2009

Vanish, Wandering Aengus Press, 2020.

Gratitude

Coaches: Jack & Nena Miller, Gary Schwabb, Ed Schindler, Don Hibler, Paul Dempsey, Jim Harney, Gary Tangen, Connie Hamilton, Dick Merenda, Al Murch, Stew MacDonald

Teammates: Queen Anne Little League, St. Margaret's CYO, QA Babe Ruth, QA Connie Mack, Seattle Prep, Shoreline CC, Western Washington University, Seattle Door, Parberry Steelers

Players: Blaine High School, Peninsula High School, Gig Harbor High School

Partners for Catch: Cam, Millers, Millers & Schaeffers— Seamus, Liam, Finnian, Maeve, Colm, & Sullivan. Barry Grimes, Jim Bodeen, John Doherty, Edwin Romond, Loren Sundlee, Rick Mark, Roland MacNichol, Don Cofer, George Mead, Vance Thompson

About the Author

Kevin Miller taught in the public schools of Washington State for thirty-nine years. He taught in Blaine, Gig Harbor, and Olympia, Washington. In 1990-1991 Miller was a Fulbright Exchange teacher at Grenå Handelsskole, Grenå, Denmark. After retirement, he was a volunteer teacher for a year at St. Patrick's School in Tacoma, Washington. Miller lives in Tacoma, Washington.

His first collection of poems, *Light That Whispers Morning*, from Blue Begonia Press received the Bumbershoot/Weyerhaeuser Publication Award in 1994. Blue Begonia Press published his second collection, *Everywhere Was Far*, in 1998. Pleasure Boat Studio published *Home & Away: The Old Town Poems* in 2009. Tacoma Arts Commission awarded him support grants for the publication of *Everywhere Was Far* and *Home & Away: The Old Town Poems*. Miller's fourth collection *Vanish* won the Wandering Aengus Press Publication Award in 2019. He was a member of the Jack Straw Writers program in 2000. Miller's poems appeared in *Heart of the Order, Persea's Baseball Anthology* in 2014; *Spitball 75*, a collection of the best poems in the first seventy-five issues of *Spitball*.

www.ingramcontent.com/pod-product-compliance
Lightning Source LLC
Chambersburg PA
CBHW030139100526
44592CB00011B/960